# JONAH and the GREAT FISH

illustrated by Leon Baxter

adapted by Belinda Hollyer

Macdonald

Everyone in ancient times had heard of the city of Nineveh. It was a rich and powerful city, and so big that you took three days to walk across it. Its streets were filled with the noise and bustle of people from all over the world. Children loved to stroke the fine silks, or dip their fingers into the strange spices, that had come from faraway lands. If they were lucky, a trader would give the children almonds or raisins to taste.

But God knew that Nineveh was a wicked city. The people there led bad lives, and they didn't even worship him properly. God wanted to help them change their ways.

'I know what I'll do,' thought God. 'I'll send Jonah to Nineveh. He can tell the people that I'm angry with them. That ought to make them behave!'

So God spoke to Jonah. 'Up you get!' he called, as Jonah rested peacefully after lunch. 'Go to Nineveh, and tell the people that I know all about their bad habits. If they don't change their ways I will destroy them; them *and* their beautiful city!'

'Bother that,' said Jonah crossly to himself. 'I don't want to go to Nineveh. If the people are so wicked, they don't deserve God's attention. In fact, they don't deserve to be saved at all! And God won't punish them if they change their ways. He'll let them off, and then my whole journey will have been a waste of time. I'm not going!'

And the next morning, instead of starting out on the road to Nineveh, Jonah crept down to the harbour. Over his shoulder was a bag of food and clothes.

'I shall run away,' he decided. 'God won't know where I am, and he'll never be able to find me. I can come back home in a while, when he's forgotten all about sending me to Nineveh!'

So Jonah found a cargo boat that was sailing to Spain. He paid his fare to the captain, sat down on the deck, and unpacked his breakfast. He felt very pleased with himself. 'I've tricked God, and I'm having a holiday as well,' he thought happily as he munched.

All that day the weather was perfect. The boat sailed across sparkling seas under a bright blue sky, and Jonah was very happy. He watched the sailors working, and talked to the other passengers. In the afternoon he dozed in the shadow of the sails, and then ate some more of his food. When evening came he found a warm, dry corner below deck for his sheepskin blanket, and curled up for the night. 'Soon I'll be in Spain,' he thought sleepily.

But God knew very well what Jonah had done, and he was angry. That night he sent a storm, and the winds blew cold and strong. The boat tossed and lurched on gigantic waves, lashed by the rain, and its timbers groaned with the strain. Soon the sails were torn to shreds by the wind. Everyone on deck was terrified.

The sailors had never seen such bad weather. They tried to steer the boat with oars, but the storm was too fierce. They were helpless. If the storm continued the boat would sink, and everyone on board would be drowned.

'Toss the cargo overboard!' shouted the captain. 'If the boat is lighter, we might ride out the storm.' So the sailors struggled below deck to get the cargo. One of them found Jonah, still sleeping, and shook him awake.

'Help us!' he yelled. 'We'll sink unless we get this cargo overboard!'

When Jonah realised what was happening he felt sick with fear. Could the storm be a sign that God was angry with him? 'Perhaps all these people are in danger because of me,' he thought as he climbed up on to the deck.

But throwing the cargo overboard didn't help. Water was now flooding the deck, and the boat was sagging dangerously with each new wave. The sailors realised that God must be angry with one of them, but they didn't know whom, or why.

'Let's draw lots,' they said. 'Whoever draws the short straw will be the one with whom God is angry.' So the captain held out a bunch of straws, with just one short straw amongst them. Everyone picked a straw. Jonah got the short straw. Now he was certain that God was punishing him for running away.

The wind howled louder as Jonah turned to the others. 'This is all my fault,' he said. 'I ran away from God, and he's angry with me. If you throw me overboard the rest of you will be saved!'

The sailors didn't want to do that. They tried again to row the boat closer to land, but they couldn't manage it. 'Are you really sure we should throw you into the water?' they asked. Jonah was sure.

'Quick!' he shouted, as the boat dived into another wave. 'You haven't got much time left! Do as I say and you'll be safe!'

So the sailors did as Jonah said. They lifted him up, carried him to the side of the boat, and dropped him into the water. He sank like a stone.

And as soon as Jonah disappeared beneath the waves the sea grew calm again. The wind dropped, and the rain stopped. The ship was safe once more, just as Jonah had said it would be.

Jonah couldn't swim, and anyway, he was too miserable to think of saving himself. His mouth and nose filled with salty water, and clammy strands of seaweed wrapped themselves around his head. In another minute he would be dead.

But just then something odd happened. Jonah couldn't see much in the dark water, but it seemed as if some enormous shape swept up to him from below. Then he felt himself sucked into a tunnel, and hurled over and over until he was dizzy. Now he was squashed, then he was stretched, and just when he thought he would never breathe again he found himself thrown on to his back in a sort of cave.

'Goodness me!' gasped Jonah. 'Where am I?' The sea had disappeared and he was trapped in a warm, sticky darkness. Jonah sat up carefully, and found that although he was bruised all over, he was certainly still alive. But where? And then he realised . . .

'Oh no, it can't be true,' he moaned. 'I must be dreaming. It's impossible!' But the impossible had really happened.

'I've been swallowed by a fish! Some enormous fish has swallowed me, and I'm standing inside its stomach!'

Jonah was glad he hadn't drowned, but it was dreadful in the fish's stomach. The smell was disgusting! Jonah had plenty of time to work out just what caused the smell. Dead fish and rotting seaweed had a lot to do with it, and so did stale seawater. Jonah couldn't keep the smell out of his nose. 'If I ever get out of here,' he thought, 'I'll never be able to eat fish again!'

There were other problems, too. Jonah was hungry, cold and wet. He didn't like the dark, and he missed the open air very much. But there was nothing he could do, and no way to escape.

On the first day, Jonah sang to himself to try to keep cheerful. On the second day he told himself stories. And on the third day, as he lay in the dark, he began to pray to God.

'I'm sorry I disobeyed you,' he said into the echoing gloom. 'If you let me out I'll do anything you ask. I'll even go to Nineveh!' But no answer came. Perhaps God had deserted him forever. What would happen to him, alone and helpless in the stomach of a fish?

But God heard Jonah, and knew that he was sorry. 'He's probably learned his lesson now,' thought God. 'I suppose I could let him out.'

So God told the fish to swim to the nearest shore. The enormous fish turned slowly in the water and headed towards the coast. It came in as close to the beach as it could. And then it opened its great mouth, stretching its jaws as wide as possible.

Inside the fish, Jonah sat up. There was light! Jonah could see the fish's mouth and teeth; and there, beyond them, a beach in the sunlight.

'Perhaps I can escape!' cried Jonah in excitement. He stumbled up the stomach, falling into pools of water and tripping over the bones, until he reached the fish's throat. Then he crept cautiously forward, wondering how to get safely past the teeth.

The fish felt Jonah's feet in its throat. They didn't hurt at all, but they did tickle. The fish shivered and wriggled, and quivered and shook. Then it could control itself no longer. With a noise that shook the sea, the fish sneezed. And Jonah flew through the teeth, sailed high into the air, and landed – smack! – on the beach.

Jonah was weak and tired, covered with seaweed and stinking of fish, but he didn't care. He could feel the warm sun on his shoulders and the sand beneath his fingers. He was safe again, back on the land where he belonged. He lay where he had fallen, breathing great gulps of fresh air. Soon, he thought, he would find the nearest town and get some food and clean clothes. And a soft, comfortable bed.

But . . .

'Up you get!' called God. 'Go to Nineveh and tell the people that I know all about their bad habits. If they don't change their ways I will destroy them; them *and* their beautiful city!'

This time Jonah went straight to Nineveh. When the people heard what God had said, they were ashamed of themselves. God saw them begin to change their ways and he was very pleased. He did not punish them after all.

When Jonah found out, he was furious. 'I knew this would happen!' he told God, stamping his foot in rage. 'Why did you tell me to come here, and then forgive them in the end? They didn't deserve to be saved!'

But God smiled. 'Oh Jonah,' he said gently, 'wouldn't you rather I forgave people when they were truly sorry?' And Jonah, remembering the fish's stomach, had to agree.

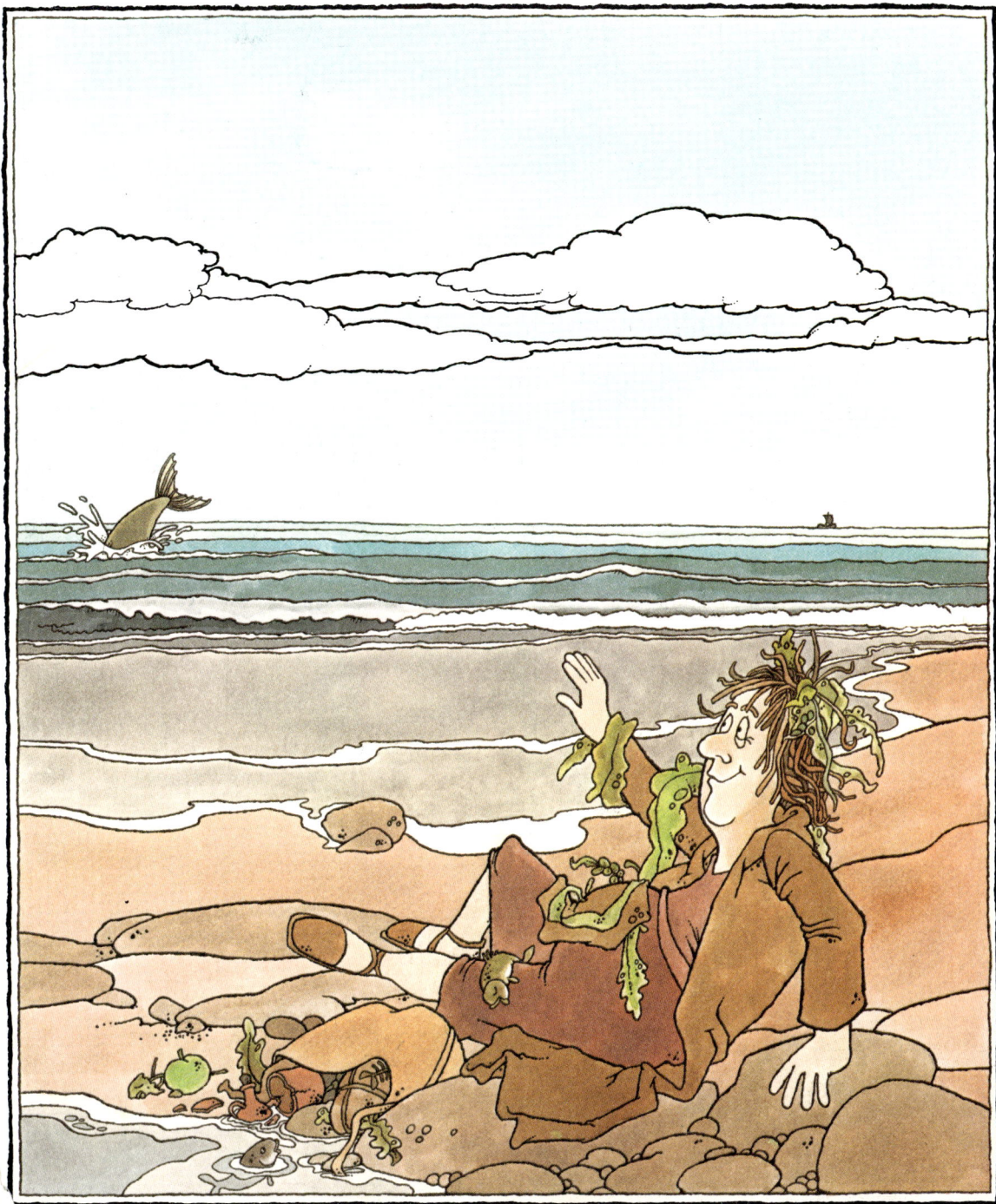

This story has been told in many different ways for more than two thousand years. It was first written down in a language called Hebrew. Since then, it has been re-told in almost every language used in the world today.

You can find the story of Jonah and the Great Fish in the Bible. It is called the Book of Jonah.